T0380672

Monday Morning Moments

Encountering Christ, one day at a time

MARIE JOYNT

WESTBOW
PRESS®
A DIVISION OF THOMAS NELSON
& ZONDERVAN

WestBow Press books may be ordered through booksellers or by contacting:

WestBow Press
A Division of Thomas Nelson & Zondervan
1663 Liberty Drive
Bloomington, IN 47403
www.westbowpress.com
844-714-3454

All Scripture quotations are taken from the Holy Bible, NEW INTERNATIONAL VERSION®, NIV® Copyright © 1973, 1978, 1984, 2011 by Biblica, Inc.® Used by permission. All rights reserved worldwide.

ISBN: 979-8-3850-2120-8 (sc)
ISBN: 979-8-3850-2121-5 (e)

Library of Congress Control Number: 2024905235

Print information available on the last page.

WestBow Press rev. date: 03/19/2024

Contents

Welcome

I was reminded of the story of Nehemiah (chapters 1–7) this morning.

Though very afraid, Nehemiah sought favor from King Artaxerxes to rebuild the walls of Jerusalem. God granted him favor as he sought the Lord, and he left for Jerusalem. Opposition came as Nehemiah was building, yet Nehemiah did not stop. The walls began to be established, and more opposition came, even death threats! Nehemiah kept building. The opposition kept pressing in, and progress was slowed as workers built with one hand and held a weapon with the other, but they kept building. They kept building!

I am so thankful to the Lord, for the many people He has blessed me with, who love me enough to redirect me. He has used different people, at specific times in my life, to help me "kick-start," give me a "shove" when needed, and always give me a loving reminder to keep building!

Monday Morning Moments has been, and will continue to be, stories of my journey with the Lord. Real life stories of ups and downs; with scrapes and bruises along the way, but also of getting up, dusting off, and continuing to build. I have been set free from chains of the past and walk in a fullness that is found in Christ alone. My sins have been forgiven by the one who was sinless and who took my sin and my shame so that I may have life to the fullest. I'm building my life upon the firm foundation that is found in Christ alone.

Sit back, grab a coffee, and journey with me as I encounter Christ, one day at a time. May God be glorified and may your hearts be encouraged.

Standing in Him,
Marie

Restorer of the Broken

I have always loved a variety of crafts; I like to knit, sew, cross-stitch, paint, and make jewelry. Another favorite pastime for me is thrift store shopping. Recently my two loves have collided and started to work as a team. I find myself at a thrift store, or sidewalk shop, searching for items that are broken, items with worn or chipped-off paint, pieces that are tired and worn out, and pieces that have been thrown to the curb as garbage. I bring home the unwanted and re-create, restore, revive, and repurpose them. The other day, I bought some old, tarnished clip-on earrings; some had stones missing, some had clips missing, and some were so tarnished they really could no longer be used as earrings. I grabbed some glue and a pair of pliers and began to repurpose these unwanted earrings into a necklace. Voilà, a masterpiece! At least in my eyes it was.

Friends, as I looked at the pile of pieces and the parts that I thought were unfixable—worthless garbage—and repurposed them into something beautiful, I was reminded that God has done the exact same thing for me! He looked down, and I handed Him *all* the pieces—all the tarnished, stained pieces. I surrender it all, with confidence, to the Master's hands, knowing I can't do anything to save and restore myself. He takes it all and restores, renews, revives, repurposes, and creates something unimaginable. I'm so thankful to God that He has the ability to look down and see the masterpiece He is creating within each of us.

God's Word reminds us in 2 Corinthians 5:17–21:

> Therefore, if anyone is in Christ, the new creation has come: The old has gone, the new is here! All this is from God, who reconciled us to himself through Christ and gave us the ministry of reconciliation: that God was

reconciling the world to himself in Christ, not counting people's sins against them. And he has committed to us the message of reconciliation. We are therefore Christ's ambassadors, as though God were making his appeal through us. We implore you on Christ's behalf: Be reconciled to God. God made him who had no sin to be sin for us, so that in him we might become the righteousness of God.

Same Road, Different Journey

In the fall of 2004, due to a change in my husband's work, we decided to move our family of four away from everything familiar. This was not a decision we made lightly. Our move would mean leaving family, wonderful friends, and a great church family; we knew we needed wisdom and guidance from the Lord before making this huge life change. The Lord was so faithful as we fasted, prayed, and sought Him. He swung the door wide open and made the next step so clear.

Not wanting our girls to transition to a new school partway through the year, we decided to move before our house sold and stay in a motel. In my human thinking, I thought, *It won't take long to sell the house, as this is the Lord's will for our family. If the Lord has made this path so clear, selling the house will be easy.* Wrong. We were going into month four at the motel. Christmas was approaching, and the house still hadn't sold. How could this be the Lord's will? *We asked You, we stepped out in faith, and now this?* A great attitude on my part, I know!

Then one day, I was driving both girls to school, and my plans were to return to the motel after and have a pity party. Christmas was right around the corner, and we were still stuck in a motel. After I dropped Erin off, I headed to the high school to drop off Amanda. As we were driving, Amanda asked, "Mom, do you remember last night when we all sat on the floor because my math books were on the little table, and we ate our Swiss Chalet chicken on the floor while watching TV?" I let her know that I did, and she replied, "Oh, Mom, are we ever going to miss times like these!"

That reply, her attitude, shook me to the core that day. You see, I wasn't the only one on this journey; Amanda was too. Transitions were hard for her, too, yet her focus was so different. She chose to see this experience as something to cherish, and in my self-pity, I got so distracted and lost my sight of it all—especially my focus on the Lord, who was still guiding, still directing, still had a plan, better than my own, even if it didn't resemble my timeline and what I wanted. That day changed my focus. I went back to that motel room and changed it into a winter wonderland; the carols were playing, and my focus was different. From that day forward, I knew that the Lord had a plan for every day we would spend in that motel, and I could trust Him.

God's Word reminds us in Isaiah 55:8–9:

> "For My thoughts are not your thoughts, neither are your ways My ways," declares the LORD. "For as the heavens are higher than the earth, so My ways are higher than your ways and my thoughts than your thoughts."

My Peace I Give You

If there was ever a time in my life that I could say I actually witnessed the peace that passes all understanding to which the Bible refers, it was in the NICU with our grandson, Matthew. God brought Matthew into this world at twenty-seven weeks of gestation. His mother, our daughter Amanda, had a case of HELLP syndrome, a life-threatening condition. Oh, how we held on to the Lord as we were at the brink of losing them both.

At one point, Amanda was at one hospital going through dialysis because her kidneys had shut down, and Matthew was in another. Amanda, regardless of how sick she was, saw Matthew every day. After Amanda got out of ICU herself, they were encouraged to do kangaroo cuddles. This meant Amanda would hold Matthew skin to skin while he was still connected to all the machines.

I would have never believed it if I hadn't witnessed it myself. While Matthew was being held, his respiration, heart rate, and oxygen levels improved dramatically. The close bonding and comfort caused this little one to come to such a peaceful stillness, it was beyond understanding. How could this baby settle and this peace come over him by just being held so close to his mom?

As someone who has struggled with anxiety and has felt heart rate and respiration increase due to anxious moments, even moments when I struggle to breathe, watching Matthew being held by his mom reminded me of what Jesus offers us. Jesus says, "Come to Me. I'm going to give you peace, and you know what else I will do? I will guard your heart and mind. I will take that anxiety and give you peace—a peace you cannot comprehend. My peace. Come, come, come to me" (Matthew 11:28).

Friend, how are you doing? Maybe today you need to snuggle into the Father, through prayer and through His Word, and experience the peace He promises.

Lessons Learned from a Hydrangea

I bought this hydrangea plant called "Endless Summer." I do love hydrangeas, and at present I have one that blooms beautiful white blooms in the spring and another that blooms beautiful rose-colored blooms in the fall. However, this hydrangea was different because it promised blooms all season long. Continuous blooms from spring to fall? Oh, how I needed this plant.

The other thing that made this hydrangea different from the two I already owned was that the color of the blooms were unknown. It would be so neat to plant this beautiful flowery shrub and wait to see the color. The greenhouse where I purchased the hydrangea enclosed a pamphlet with gardening tips and such. The pamphlet stated that the color of the blooms depended on the soil in which the hydrangea was planted. What was inside, and hidden in the ground, would determine the color of the blossoms.

This made me think about my own life. It made me think about the soil of my own heart. What was deep in the soil of my heart, and what was that soil producing outwardly? I can say with certainty that when my heart has held on to bitterness, unforgiveness, anger, and resentment, the outward blossoms usually produced were hurtful words or actions.

So what does the soil of your heart look like, friend? What kinds of blossoms are being produced by it?

God's Word reminds us in Luke 6:45:

> A good man brings good things out of the good stored up in his heart,
> and an evil man brings evil things out of the evil stored up in his heart.
> For the mouth speaks what the heart is full of.

Prayer

Lord, we ask that You reveal the condition of the soil in our hearts. May we be like David and cry out, "Create in me a clean heart, oh God, and renew a right spirit within me" (Psalm 51:10). Lord, may our hearts' soil be rich in love, kindness, and gentleness, and may that be expressed through our words and deeds. Amen.

In the Presence of a Holy God

I have found that when I slow down in my Bible reading and focus on a smaller portion by rereading and making notes, I am able to obtain more from the text. As I studied Isaiah 5 and 6, I found this to be true, and I was left with the question, "What happened to the prophet Isaiah from chapter 5 to chapter 6?" In Isaiah 5, Isaiah repeatedly says, "Woe to you." However, in chapter 6, Isaiah says, "Woe to me." What caused Isaiah to take his focus off the others' hearts and sins and place the focus on himself instead? Isaiah had an encounter with a holy God. This shook Isaiah to the core: "'Woe to me!' I cried. 'I am ruined! For I am a man of unclean lips, and I live among a people of unclean lips, and my eyes have seen the King, the Lord Almighty'" (Isaiah 6:5 NIV).

Isaiah was standing in the presence of a holy God—a God to be exalted and a God to be feared. In the presence of a holy God, Isaiah's heart was exposed, and the prophet thought the only fair outcome was for him to be consumed and ruined. But God is gracious, and instead of Isaiah being consumed, he was cleansed and his sins atoned for (Isaiah 6:5–7).

What about you? When you think of God, does your heart tend to rest in His character trait of love? I rested in that mindset for years. "God is love" was used to cover my tracks, or rest, in a forever safety net of my repetitive sin cycles. Now don't get me wrong. God is love, but above all else, the character of God I have been drawn to and reminded of often is that God is holy. When we come into an encounter with a holy God, all is exposed before Him. We can't help but see ourselves and examine our hearts.

Friend, have you come into the presence of a Holy God? I am reminded and humbled as I read Romans 14:11: "It is written: 'As surely as I live,' says the Lord, 'every knee will bow before me; every tongue will acknowledge God.'"

Quenching a Thirst

One day I went to the gym—strong emphasis on the one! I wasn't familiar with working out or the variety of equipment I would be using. I also went into that day having no idea how much I would need water. I could not believe how thirsty I became as I worked out. I can truly say I have never been that thirsty ever. As soon as I arrived home, do you think I grabbed a large glass of cold water or a bowl of salty popcorn to satisfy that thirst? Why would the salty popcorn be a bad decision for someone who was thirsty?

The Bible tells a story of a woman who had a deep thirst. She was the talk of the town. She specifically drew water at a time of day that no one would be there. The other women would gather at the well, visit and socialize, but she came alone. With her head hung low, she walked toward the well only to encounter Him. Chance? I think not, more like ordained by our heavenly Father. Jesus addresses and confronts her thirst that day. He satisfies it in a way that she would have never imagined. Her thirst was satisfied in Him, and she couldn't wait to tell others.

Take the time to read this story of a thirsty, transformed heart in John 4:4–38. The story unfolds with a Samaritan woman who had a thirst that wasn't satisfied until she met Jesus. She tried to fill those voids, those gaps in her life, with everything but Him.

Oh friend, this sounds all too familiar. Oh how we hunger and thirst to be filled by approval, jobs, status, wealth, and success. We have this deep longing and void and keep trying to fill it with everything but Him.

Do you thirst today?

Friends, let's journey to the well. Let's meet Him there to satisfy our longings and our thirsts. Come, all you who are thirsty, and you will be satisfied.

Today I Saw a Downy Woodpecker!

Okay, I can hear some of you already ... "who cares, big deal, what's a downy woodpecker?" I understand, and I would probably say the same thing, but you need to hear the back story. Two years ago, I purchased this feeder. This bird feeder was specifically made to attract woodpeckers. I had purchased the specific peanuts that were recommended, and I waited and waited and waited. My daughter had an identical feeder, and she had tons of bird activity. Why was I not getting the same results? I had waited two years, and it wasn't working. Last week, as I was filling up all my feeders, I went over to this feeder and decided to remove it. I was discouraged and ready to throw in the towel; there were no downy woodpeckers in Haldimand County. It was then that I saw the downy woodpecker.

Can you relate to this story? While you may not be waiting on a downy woodpecker, are you waiting on something or someone? Are you getting discouraged? Are you feeling defeated and just want to throw in the towel?

Sometimes we can find ourselves waiting. We don't understand why, how long, or when this waiting will end. However, as a child of God we can be confident that God is in complete control of our waiting experience. He is with you in the waiting, and His plans are always for His glory and our good.

Friend, I know how difficult the waiting can be. I know that in the waiting we can express a wide range of emotions and fears; the waiting can be very difficult.-Christ himself can understand and sympathize with us in the waiting. I'm praying for you today to feel His presence and peace surrounding you as you wait.

God's word reminds us in Psalm 130:5: "I wait for the LORD, my soul does wait, and in His word do I hope."

Early Detection Is Key

Being married to a tree guy, also known as an arborist, our car trips involve looking at a lot of vegetation along the route. Recently, my husband, Dan, was preparing a PowerPoint presentation at work on the effects of emerald ash borer. I had heard of emerald ash borer, but I was shocked to learn about the thousands of healthy ash trees it was wiping out. What shocked me most was the tiny little D-shaped hole on the tree that was responsible for all the devastation. While the tree from the outside was luscious and green, when you peeled back the bark the entire tree was rotten. Dan explained to me that the only way of saving the tree was early detection of this tiny little, destructive, deadly beast.

This got me thinking about our spiritual lives and how the tiny things left unchecked are allowed to fester in our lives. Tiny things like: unforgiveness, bitterness, anger, jealousy, pride, or greed. When I read Galatians 5:13–26, it challenged me to get rid of anything within me that may be slowly eating away. This required me to ask the Lord to allow the Holy Spirit to guide me so that my life would bear much fruit.

Prayer

Heavenly Father, you are such a merciful, forgiving Father. Thank you for your word, which reminds us that if we confess our sins, you are so faithful and just and will forgive us from all unrighteousness. Thank you for giving each believer the help of the Holy Spirit. May we walk with the Spirit, as He guides and directs us, that we may be able to see the areas in our lives that would benefit from early detection—things that don't please or resemble You and need to be rooted out. May Your word continue to shape us and challenge us to live lives led by the Spirit. May we reflect You this day by living self-controlled lives, extending love, joy, peace, and being kind and patient to others. Amen.

Staying Focused in the Storm

It was a beautiful, sunny summer day. and the camp our nine-year-old daughter, Erin, was attending had decided it was a perfect day to canoe across the lake. The day was running along nicely, and after lunch all campers and leaders boarded their canoes and started heading back to camp. While they were out in the middle of the lake, a terrible storm blew in out of nowhere. It was a hailstorm and rainstorm like no other. I remember it well because I was with my other daughter, Amanda, having lunch at a coffee shop. Looking out the window, we could not get over how dark the day turned and how quickly the storm came. It was a severe and damaging storm that resulted in car dealerships having to put in insurance claims for damage. My mother's heart had immediately thought of Erin but never imagined that Erin was out in this storm. Amanda and I were going to take refuge in the coffee shop and then head back to camp.

When we had returned to camp, unaware that Erin had been out on the lake, the last canoe had just been accounted for. All campers were safely onshore; the tears, the fears, the excitement, the hugging, and the thankfulness were loud and buzzing. As we were listening to the stories, one little girl said to me, "It was so bad and we were so scared, and we started to pray," and then she paused and said with a trembling voice, "and when we started to pray, it got worse!"

Oh, how often does this happen? We take a stand, we pray, we hand it over to God, and we claim our absolute trust in Him, and then, because we are impatient or expect the prayer to be answered immediately, we start to flounder when it isn't. We begin to doubt God and fear as the raging storm, which seems more powerful than God, is surrounding us.

We cannot forget, while the storm rages on, that God is not only with us but is using the storm to grow us. The Bible associates many storms with spiritual growth. We see this in Matthew 14:22–23. When Peter found himself in the middle of a storm, there was fear, but Jesus was there. When Peter focused and fixed his eyes on Christ, he was drawing nearer to Him; but when Peter focused on the storm, he began to be overwhelmed with fear and sink. Where are you fixing your eyes in your storms?

Real or Counterfeit?

When my husband and I were first married, we moved for his job, so I got a job as a teller in the local bank. It was a small-town bank, and I so enjoyed the job and just getting to know the people in this community. Our small-town bank didn't have the problem that other banks had with counterfeit bills, but we did get to see and touch counterfeit bills to distinguish the difference.

Years ago, if a teller took in a counterfeit bill, he or she was responsible to reimburse the bank. This meant that knowing the difference between real and counterfeit was key, as it could truly cost you! The best way to know or expose a counterfeit was not to examine various counterfeits but to know the real thing. If you are familiar with the real thing, a counterfeit will stand out like a beacon shining in a dark night.

The same applies to us as believers. The more we know the truth, the more we can distinguish the lies. In God's word we see, in both the Old and New Testament, that we have a real enemy of our souls—the devil. As a child of God the enemy hates us and what we stand for and will do anything to discourage or discredit our witness for Christ.

God's word warns us the devil is deceptive. He prowls seeking whom he may devour. He is a slanderer and has come to kill, steal, and destroy. He is the accuser of the brethren, and he attempts to accuse us before God and ourselves.

God's word is true; He cannot lie. God's word will expose the lies and shine light on truth and will equip us to stand firm. God's word empowers us to resist the enemy and stand firm in our faith. When we do this, the enemy must flee.

Additional insight in God's word:

Ephesians 6:10–20
John 1:14, 4:24, 8:32, 10:10, 14:6, 16:13, 17:17

Lessons Learned from Painting a Door

I knew our front door needed painting, but I didn't realize how in need it was until we had purchased a new screen door. Once the new screen door was up, it was clear how badly our front door needed to be painted! It didn't take me long to realize that while I love DIY projects, I do not like painting! I like purchasing the paint and brushes and leaving the paint by the back door for Danny. I do love the finished product but do not like the steps leading up to it.

What I also realized as I was repainting our white door was that the door really wasn't white at all. What I thought was a white door was actually more of a yellow than white. The years had striped the white door of its once brilliant shine and left behind a dingy version of itself. How come I didn't realize how yellow this door was? How did I miss it changing over the years right before my eyes?

The Lord understands us all so perfectly. For me, He knows that I can draw applications through the daily tasks I complete. As I sat painting our front door, it really wasn't about the paint anymore but about my own life. I was left pondering: What has grown dingy in my life? What has faded over time?

So the question is, what is your front door? What is growing dingy in your life or changing right before your very eyes, and you can't see it? Not all change is bad, but is there change in your life that is not drawing you closer to the Lord and changing you in a way that brings you in more likeness with Jesus?

Prayer

"Search me, God, and know my heart; test me and know my anxious thoughts. See if there is any offensive way in me and lead me in the way everlasting" (Psalm 139:23–24).

Let Me Drive

When it came time to teach our girls to drive, it had to be my husband to take them. Let's just say I am not the best passenger. Truth is I would rather be the one driving. Not that I felt I was a better driver but just felt better being in control of the steering wheel.

The problem with the let-me-drive mentality is that it often has crossed over to my relationship with my heavenly Father. It isn't really about driving at all but rather about being in control.

Many times I find I'm the one trying to direct the Lord to my path, my plans, my way. When I am in the driver's seat, I can choose the smooth road with no hills or valleys. It's so difficult at times to release the tight grip I hold onto that steering wheel, in certain areas of my life, and to just trust Him, listen to Him and just be guided by Him and let Him drive.

I find the sooner I release my tight grip on that steering wheel and push pride aside, by humbling myself and surrendering whatever circumstance I am in to Him, He directs, guides, and brings peace into that area. I have also experienced that once I totally surrender my heart to Him, I am more aligned with His heart, His plan, and His will. This process of handing him the steering wheel is not always easy, but the more I meditate on His word, seek His heart and His way through prayer, it becomes easier to surrender that wheel and let Him drive.

God's word reminds us in Proverbs 3:5–6: "Trust in the Lord with all your heart, and lean not on your own understanding; in all your ways acknowledge him, and he will direct your path."

"The gatekeeper opens the gate for him, and the sheep listen to his voice. He calls his own sheep by name and leads them out. When he has brought out all his own, he goes on ahead of them, and his sheep follow him because they know his voice" (John 10:3–4).

The Master Weaver

A dear friend of mine gave me a bookmark last week, and inscribed on it was this poem:

My life is but a weaving between my God and me, I do not choose the colors, He works so steadily. Oftentimes He weaves in sorrow, and I in foolish pride, forget He sees the upper, and I the underside. Not till the loom is silent, and the shuttle ceases to fly, will God unroll the canvas and explain the reasons why. The dark threads are as needful in the weavers skillful hand, as the threads of gold and silver in the pattern He has planned. ("The Weaver," by Grant Colfax Tullar)

I think of the many times I have looked up into the heavens and cried out, "God, what are you doing?" I have questioned His timing on things, or, if I'm being honest, I have just truly wanted the smooth road, the road with no suffering, no pain, no bumps or sharp turns. Over the years, I have seen that it has been those dark threads He has woven into my tapestry that have truly drawn me closer to Him. Those dark threads have grown me and stretched me in my faith.

Those dark threads, that I would have never chosen, have always been used for my good and His glory! I'm thankful and rest in the One who weaves and continues to weave the various threads in my life; while it isn't always easy, the master weaver knows what He is doing.

More promises from the Master Weaver:

James 1:2–4

1 Peter 1:3–8

Proverbs 3:5–6

Jeremiah 29:11–12

2 Corinthians 12:9

Romans 8: 28

Lessons Learned from a Tree Stand

My husband's love language is quality time, and time spent in the woods and hunting is icing on the cake, and that is how I found myself sitting high up in a tree. It's cold, it's windy, and it seems like hours that I'm waiting. Then to my left I see a large female deer approaching. She was so quiet that it caught me off guard. I wasn't ready, and she came in from a direction I wasn't expecting. She also came way closer than I had thought.

Nothing was going according to plan, and my heart started to race. The crossbow seemed to weigh two hundred pounds, as I lifted it into position. I watched her walk closer, but she saw me, and I couldn't get a shot. She flicked her tail and ran … I shot … I missed. Then, to my shock, she came back. I couldn't believe it; I now had the perfect shot and couldn't take it. If only I had been patient and waited. I sat there and watched her for over fifteen minutes. I couldn't shoot because, without help, I do not have the physical strength to get my crossbow into position to fire it again. If only I had waited!

The next two hours up in the tree, waiting for my Danny to return, I had a lot of time to reflect. I sensed the Lord say, "Marie, it's not about the deer. How many times do you, in your lack of patience, run ahead of Me? How often do you insist on your way, your timing, and just barge through and not wait on Me?" Oh friends, I could remember far too many times in that moment that I have not waited, and I could also recall the consequences because I had not waited on the Lord and trusted His timing in it all.

What about you? You are sitting in God's waiting room, and you are crying out, "How long, Lord?" As you wait, you see others come and go, and you continue waiting.

Waiting on a spouse, waiting on a job, waiting on a loved one to come to Christ, waiting on improved health. Whatever you are waiting on, the wait can be long and difficult, but He is waiting with you.

Great reminders in the waiting room:

Isaiah 40:31, 30:18
Psalm 25:4–5, 27:13–14, 33:20–22
Proverbs 3:5–6
Lamentations 3:25

Read the Manual

Christmas Eve 1976, my little sister was six years old, and Holly Hobby was all the rage. As she said good night to us at around eight thirty that evening, we knew the night had only begun for us. My mom had ordered a Holly Hobby house from the Sears Christmas Wish Book, and our job that evening was to help assemble it with Mom. How hard could this be? Mom had three teenagers that were committed to helping her. I was twelve at the time and just so excited thinking about my sister's reaction in the morning, as I pulled pieces out of this big box.

My mom started to read the instruction manual. We thought we found the pieces the manual had suggested, but they didn't fit, so Mom went back to the manual and then back again to recheck and so on and so on. By this time, my older brother had had it and suggested we just duct tape this house together. I remember my mom just suggesting he head to bed, and we would endure. Mom pushed through that evening, continuing to check the manual, and by around 2:00 a.m. the house was standing. It looked amazing, and not a piece of duct tape was used.

This memory reminded me of an acronym I heard one time for the word *Bible*, and it was: Basic Instructions Before Leaving Earth.

I don't know about you, but I need to return to this manual, the Bible, often. I need to be reminded who God is, His promises, and who I am as a child of His. This manual brings me peace when the storm is raging. It brings me comfort, clarity, and direction when I feel alone. This book corrects me and calls my sinful heart to repentance. This book restores my soul and refreshes my heart. But, above all else, this book keeps me focused on Him.

The psalmist who wrote Psalm 119 realizes the importance of giving glory to God and His word. I'm confident He checked the manual often.

Take a peek at some of the encouragement found in Psalm 119.

Light in the Darkness

Our two-and-a-half-year-old grandson, Matthew, has had this fascination lately with being in the dark. The bathroom at their house has no window at all, so when you shut the door, and the lights are not on, it is pitch black. He often runs inside and shuts the door. The other day he ran inside the bathroom and called his mommy to come in with him. On this particular day, when he shut the door and as he stood in complete darkness he said, "Oh, no! I can't see Matthew." This was followed by, "Mommy, please help!" His mommy immediately turned on the light. For whatever reason, that day the lack of light frightened him, and he called out for help, and his mom quickly changed that darkness to light with a flip of a switch.

God's word has so many reminders of darkness and light, and I'm so thankful to God for rescuing me from that dominion of darkness (in which I once walked) into His glorious light.

> For God, who said, "Light shall shine out of darkness," is the One who has shone in our hearts to give the Light of the knowledge of the glory of God in the face of Christ. (2 Corinthians 4:6)

> But you are a chosen race, a royal priesthood, a holy nation, a people for God's own possession, so that you may proclaim the excellencies of Him who has called you out of darkness into His marvelous light. (1 Peter 2:9)

> For you were formerly darkness, but now you are Light in the Lord; walk as children of Light. (Ephesians 5:8)

Then Jesus again spoke to them, saying, "I am the Light of the world; he who follows Me will not walk in the darkness, but will have the Light of life." (John 8:12)

"To open their eyes so that they may turn from darkness to light and from the dominion of Satan to God, that they may receive forgiveness of sins and an inheritance among those who have been sanctified by faith in Me." (Acts 26:18)

Me and My Stinkin' Thinkin'

I did not realize until God started to gently strip away things in my life that I didn't resemble Him. My thinking had to change. Oh, what a negative thinker I was! I was always thinking about the worst possible scenario or outcome. That thinking was not from God at all, and my thinking had to change. I had to start taking seriously the renewing of my mind in Christ and start thinking biblically in all circumstances and situations.

In God's word, Paul often refers to being transformed by the renewing of our minds. The mind is so key in our Christian walk. Our minds must be transformed from our sinful flesh nature to a mindset focused on Christ. Paul challenges us in Colossians 2:6–7 that just as you received Christ, so walk in Him. As we walk in Him, we must be setting our hearts and minds on things above. Our ungodly ways of thinking must change into new biblical ways of thinking … thinking with the mind of Christ.

So how do I start thinking with the mind of Christ? The word of God is pretty specific and even gives a list found in Philippians 4:8: "Finally, brothers and sisters, whatever is true, whatever is noble, whatever is right, whatever is pure, whatever is lovely, whatever is admirable—if anything is excellent or praiseworthy—think about such things."

When a worry, fear, or an anxious thought comes, we who have been given the mind of Christ have the ability, with the help of the Holy Spirit, to push that out of our minds and replace it with a godly thought. Trust me, this takes practice, but with persistence and the help from the Holy Spirit, it gets easier, and you will walk in freedom and peace.

So what are we thinking about? What are we dwelling on? Our battle will be won or lost in the mind. The struggle against worry, anxiety, negative thinking, and fear is a battle for the mind. That's why Paul tells believers so clearly what we are to think about in Philippians 4:8.

Lessons Learned on a Soccer Field

It was a bright, sunny afternoon, and my little niece (nine years old) was playing in a soccer game, and she was goalie. Oh no, not the goalie! Everyone either loves or hates the goalie; there seems to be no in-between. That day she had three family member cheerleaders: her mom, her grandmother, and her older cousin. The game wasn't going very well, and goal after goal was getting in. When the coach called a time-out, my niece didn't run to the huddle; she ran to her family and said, "It's really bad; we are losing, and I can't hear you. You have to cheer louder!" She knew the importance of encouragement, and she knew she needed extra help and support. As they cheered louder, the confidence they saw in her was noticeable and while the game wasn't won, a great lesson was learned.

The Bible reminds us of a story, not on a soccer field but a battlefield. It is found in Exodus 17:8–13.

> The Amalekites came and attacked the Israelites at Rephidim. Moses said to Joshua, "Choose some of our men and go out to fight the Amalekites. Tomorrow I will stand on top of the hill with the staff of God in my hands." So Joshua fought the Amalekites as Moses had ordered, and Moses, Aaron and Hur went to the top of the hill. As long as Moses held up his hands, the Israelites were winning, but whenever he lowered his hands, the Amalekites were winning. When Moses' hands grew tired, they took a stone and put it under him and he sat on it. Aaron and Hur held his hands up—one on one side, one on the other—so that his hands

remained steady till sunset. So Joshua overcame the Amalekite army with the sword. (Exodus 17:8–13)

Just like Moses needed help, we need each other. Who are you cheering on? Who are you holding up while they endure battle? Who are you persevering with through prayer? Who are you helping and comforting with the same comfort you have received from God in your time of need? If no one comes to mind, go before the Lord in prayer and ask the Lord to fill your heart with someone who you can cheer on and encourage this week.

Blessings, dear friend, as you encourage one another and build each other up.

Closet Makeover

My mom recently came for a visit and brought me a brand-new pair of moccasins. These were beautiful moccasins, which I was so thankful to get. My old pair was worn out; they had holes in the bottom of them, tears on the side and most of the fur was missing. These old moccasins were also stained, stretched out of shape, and larger than the size of my feet now. They were stinky, old, ripped, worn-out slippers ready for the garbage.

Oh, I loved these new moccasins! They were so comfortable, and I was so thankful to receive them. The next day, as I crawled out of bed and reached to grab my slippers, which pair do you think I put on? They were both there, sitting beside each other. Believe it or not, I put on the old, stinky, torn, ready for the garbage pair! Why would I do that? Why would I choose the old, when I was gifted with the new, and they were sitting right there? Was it out of habit? Why didn't I put on the new?

In the book of Colossians, Paul is addressing the Church of Colossae with the same kind of question (not about stinky footwear). He is stressing in the letter the importance of their new identity that is found in Christ and not to continue to put on the old but to put on the new.

With closet doors wide open, let's walk in and put on the new; the Lord is calling us to. Take a moment and read Colossians 3:1–17.

Now it's your turn; in response to God's word and what you have learned, what articles are in your closet right now that you know do not belong in there as a chosen child of God? What steps are you going to take this week regarding a closet makeover?

Prayer

Heavenly Father, thank you! Thank you for your love and the grace you have shown me. Lord, I confess that many times I have not put on what I am called to put on as your chosen child. Forgive me for the many times I have put on things or spoken things that do not resemble you. Holy Spirit, I ask for your guidance, wisdom, and strength to put on love. In Jesus's name I pray, *amen*.

Chipping Away One Piece at a Time

My husband, Danny, loves to carve and create. We have many beautiful, small carvings that he has worked on over the years displayed in our home. A few years back he wanted to attempt something bigger, so my brother Coleman brought Danny and I down this beautiful basswood beam he had cut and milled off his property back home. Danny had a great vision for this beam; he wanted to carve out a scene and make it into a beautiful mantle for a fireplace we would eventually put in our living room. Like any carving project in the past that Danny had done, it takes tons of patience and lots of time. So Dan began to chip away. Danny knew what he wanted to see as the end result, yet it was taking so long to get there. Many months later, a beautiful piece of art!

It got me thinking about my relationship with my heavenly Father and how He has many times, with chisel in hand, chipped away anything that did not resemble Him. There have been many times he has chipped away big pieces that had no beauty at all, like various sins, anger, jealousy, or pride. God's word directs us and encourages us to chip away those things too (Colossians 3:1–17, Galatians 5:13–26).

Unlike this mantel, I have many more years of being chipped away by the Master's hand. But as I fix my eyes on Him, seek Him above all else, daily spend time with Him in prayer and the studying of His word, He will bring to light the things that don't resemble Him. My heart's desire is to resemble the beauty that He has always seen in me from the first day He started chipping away to make me more like Him.

For today's prayer time, use the scriptures below to pray God's word over yourself:

Psalm 139:23–24, 51:10

Business Card Gospel

We just had some work done on our sunroom at the lake. The sunroom was leaking in at least four areas of the roof, so we knew we had to get on top of this. We hired a young man who had done a roof job for us previously. When we arrived at the lake the roof was completed, and Carl had left us our invoice, business card, and a few complimentary pens. I was touched when I flipped over his business card and saw how Carl chose to pay the extra money to have a two-sided business card, and on the other side he chose to share the hope he had found in Jesus. The back of Carl's business card had John 14:6: "Jesus says to us, 'I am the way, the truth and the life.'"

I immediately was reminded of a pastor friend of ours who shared with us, when he wasn't a believer and was working in the corporate world that he was trying to save this company money by suggesting they go to a one-sided business card. However, the corporate CEO he had worked for had chosen, like Carl did, to share a message of hope on his business cards too. When our friend went to the CEO, he shared about Christ and over the months led our friend to the Lord. A changed, transformed life because of a seed of hope on a business card. Where are you planting seeds of hope? Where are you taking opportunities to share the hope that you have found?

God's word reminds us:

> As the rain and the snow come down from heaven and do not return to it without watering the earth and making it bud and flourish, so that it yields seed for the sower and bread for the eater, so is my word that goes out from my mouth: It will not return to me empty, but will

accomplish what I desire and achieve the purpose for which I sent it. (Isaiah 55:10–11)

But in your hearts revere Christ as Lord. Always be prepared to give an answer to everyone who asks you to give the reason for the hope that you have. (1 Peter 3:15)

Looking on the Inside

We just changed and updated our kitchen. The old oak cupboards were still in great shape yet looked a little dated, so we painted them. We also decided to take the wood panels out of two of the doors and put in glass.

Here is where the dilemma came—what will we put in those cupboards with the glass doors? Whatever we choose to put in these cupboards all can see; the contents of the other cupboards are not revealed. I had two terribly messy junk drawers and a cupboard with plastic containers that could avalanche at any given moment, but they were hidden; they were not exposed like these two new cupboards with glass. What should we put in these exposed cupboards? Do we just put some pretty decorative items? What to do!

I immediately saw a parallel to my own heart and life. I was reminded that no matter how hard I may work on the outside and what man may see—God is the one that sees the heart—and God will judge the heart. I realize I even expose my own heart and what is truly inside me when I am squeezed, angered, or pressed in on—what is truly inside will come out.

What about you? Did you shutter at the thought of all being exposed? Did a sin or a situation come to mind that you have tucked away and hidden?

God's Word reminds us:

> The LORD does not look at the things people look at. People look at the outward appearance, but the LORD looks at the heart. (1 Samuel 16:7b)

Nothing in all creation is hidden from God's sight. Everything is uncovered and laid bare before the eyes of him to whom we must give account. (Hebrews 4:13)

Wait until the Lord comes. He will bring to light what is hidden in darkness and will expose the motives of the heart. (1 Corinthians 4:5b)

Friend, may the Lord direct your heart how to respond to His word today.

Nip It In the Bud!

I don't know about you, but I have a lot of sayings that I have carried with me since I was young. A few stand out to me from childhood, and I can still hear my mother saying, "Nip it in the bud." My mother also said (often) to me, "Make sure your sins will find you out." Well, both of those sayings kind of collided when I looked at this plant in our daughters' room the other day. This was our daughter Erin's plant, and it was a beautiful, green, healthy bamboo plant. This plant, when tended to and remembered, continued to flourish. Since Erin got married, I remembered the odd time to tend it but more often forgot to care for it. About two months ago I saw the root of one shoot turning yellow, and I actually contemplated removing this whole section of the yellow, decayed shoot, but I didn't. Instead, I did a quick little water and fed it and then left it.

With the busyness of life in general and this plant not being a priority, I was shocked to see what had happened over the past two months. This once flourishing, healthy plant was contaminated from the root up. This plant was now more yellow and dead than green and flourishing. Oh, why didn't I *nip it in the bud?* I saw it needed more care, but I left it.

I ask you, is there anything trying to take root in your heart or mind? Is there any activity or habit in your life that is taking root that should be nipped? Is busyness keeping you so distracted that you are not tending to and feeding your soul? I'm drawn to this passage of scripture where Jesus is speaking to his disciples:

> "Remain in me, as I also remain in you. No branch can bear fruit by itself; it must remain in the vine. Neither can you bear fruit unless you remain in me. I am the vine; you are the branches. If you remain in

me and I in you, you will bear much fruit; apart from me you can do nothing. If you do not remain in me, you are like a branch that is thrown away and withers; such branches are picked up, thrown into the fire and burned." (John 15:4–6)

Friends, apart from Him we can't do it. Abiding in Him will expose any roots that are not of Him, abiding in Him and in His word is life. Take some time right now and come into His presence. Ask Him what may need to be nipped out of your life and practical ways you can keep abiding.

Touched but Not Changed

A parable is told of a community of ducks waddling off to duck church one Sunday to hear their duck preacher. After they waddled into the duck sanctuary, the service began, and the duck preacher spoke eloquently of how God had given the ducks wings with which to fly. He pounded the pulpit with his beak and said, "With these wings, there is no where we ducks cannot go! There is no God-given task we ducks cannot accomplish! With these wings we no longer need to walk through life. We can soar high in the sky!" Shouts of "Amen!" were quacked throughout the duck congregation. The duck preacher concluded his message by exclaiming, "God has given us wings! *We … can … fly!*" More ducks quacked out loud *"amens!"* in response. Every duck loved the service; in fact, all the ducks that were present commented on what a wonderfully encouraging and convicting message they had heard from their duck preacher. Every duck felt so empowered and encouraged by the message … and then when it was time to leave the church … they *all* waddled home. (Soren Kierkegaard)

I remember a season in my life, a season of complacency when I would waddle off the same way that I waddled in, week after week after week. Going through the motions, serving, working in my own strength … touched but not changed and exhausted. I would read in God's word of being "more than a conqueror," (Romans 8:37) and most days just feeling tired, weary, and defeated. The complacency only started to change when I began to discipline myself to be daily in God's word, meditate on scripture, apply the word to my life, spend time in prayer and seeking Him above all else.

The waddling started to leave when I allowed the word of God and the work of the Holy Spirit to begin to transform my heart and mind in Christ Jesus. Then I started to walk in the power and authority I was given as a beloved child of the Most High. Each time you sit under a teaching or open the word of God, come expecting, come with teachable hearts, ears attentive, hands open, ready to receive from the Almighty (James 1:22–25, 2 Timothy 3:16–17).

Who Are You Listening To?

The water ran down around the altar and even filled the trench. At the time of sacrifice, the prophet Elijah stepped forward and prayed: "Lord, the God of Abraham, Isaac and Israel, let it be known today that you are God in Israel and that I am your servant and have done all these things at your command. Answer me, Lord, answer me, so these people will know that you, Lord, are God, and that you are turning their hearts back again." Then the fire of the Lord fell and burned up the sacrifice, the wood, the stones and the soil, and also licked up the water in the trench. When all the people saw this, they fell prostrate and cried, "The Lord—he is God! The Lord—he is God!" (1 Kings 18:35–39)

Now let's fast-forward just a little bit:

Now Ahab told Jezebel everything Elijah had done and how he had killed all the prophets with the sword. So, Jezebel sent a messenger to Elijah to say, "May the gods deal with me, be it ever so severely, if by this time tomorrow I do not make your life like that of one of them." Elijah was afraid and ran for his life … He came to a broom bush, sat down under it and prayed that he might die. "I have had enough, Lord," he said. "Take my life; I am no better than my ancestors." (1 Kings 19:1–4)

What happened here? What happened to this powerful prophet of God? He just witnessed an amazing act of God and now has hit the wall, runs away, trembling with fear and just wants to die. Shocking how one sentence from Jezebel shook this strong man of God ... one sentence! Have you been there? I have! I have watched the Lord part the waters and move the mountains in some pretty hopeless situations and then I get tripped up in believing a lie, and I tremble in fear, lose my focus, question God, and it can spiral down pretty quickly from there.

Prayer

Lord please forgive us for those times we take our eyes off You. Forgive us for those many times we question You, doubt You, and believe lies. Thank You for the grace You show us in the times that we are faithless; You remain faithful. Lord, please continue to lead us into all truth. Amen.

A Storm Is Coming

A big winter storm is coming, that was all that I seemed to hear last week. Whether in the bank line, the dentist office, at the grocery store ... it's not like we haven't had snowstorms here, but this winter we have not really had to endure much of winter at all; it has been quite lovely and comfortable. But now this storm was coming and was going to change those spring-like comfort days and people were talking and preparing, and the weatherman confirmed it. This storm was on its way, and you better be ready.

Saturday morning, when the storm was said to hit, I was to be leading worship at a women's conference at our home church. My main preparation for the storm was to arrange to stay closer to the church, so I would not be driving in the bad storm. That evening, I stayed at my daughter's home. I woke around 3:00 a.m., and I was wide awake (some of you ladies can relate to that). I knew I needed my rest for the full day that lay ahead.

I am learning in those times to trust God as He knows I need my rest but to seek Him in that time and pray for others. During this quiet time with the Lord, it came upon my heart how people were preparing for this storm that was coming. How people were believing the weatherman and the weather reports and were getting ready. It was like the Lord said in that quiet time, "Where is the urgency regarding Me? How are you preparing for My return? Are you telling others about Me with the same urgency you are about this storm?"

My heart and my response were shaken to the core at that moment. Jesus is coming back. Do I have the urgency about that that I do regarding other things? Have I told others of Him with love, compassion, and urgency? Friends, God's word reminds us

He is coming soon; we are to be ready for His triumphant return. No one will know the day or time, but He is coming! Are you ready?

Many of us believed the weatherman's prediction of the storm. Trust me, God's word is truth, no error or mistake. We can trust Him with confidence. He is coming. Are you ready? (Matthew 16:27, 24:36, 24:42; Luke 12:40; Revelation 3:3, 1:7).

A Distracted Heart

As Jesus and his disciples were on their way, He came to a village where a woman named Martha opened her home to him. She had a sister called Mary who sat at the Lord's feet listening to what he said. But Martha was distracted by all the preparations that had to be made and she came to Him and asked, "Lord, don't you care that my sister has left me to do the work by myself? Tell her to help me!"

"Martha, Martha," the Lord answered, "you are worried and upset about many things but few things are needed—or indeed only one thing is necessary. Mary has chosen what is better and it will not be taken away from her." (Luke 10:38–42)

Life is full of distractions, and Martha was distracted. The literal meaning of the word means she was being drawn in different directions. Distractions can damage relationships; they hinder our listening, they rob us of being still—to pray, to meditate, and to read God's word. Martha was distracted. She was serving, she was doing good things, but what she was doing was not the problem. The problem lay within her heart. Martha's heart was distracted and was in turmoil. When our hearts get consumed with our distractions, things can spiral pretty quickly.

Recently, I was confronted with this in my quiet time with the Lord. I had a distracted heart. I could say I was just busy, but I was focused on a bazillion different things and pulled in all directions—my small business, my social media accounts, my phone, my family, the holidays. I could make a great fighting argument for all of them, but my distractions were taking a toll. My distractions were like the 3rd soil that is mentioned in Luke 8 where the planted seed is being choked by life's worries, pleasures, or riches. I don't know whether you have felt this way, but after time in prayer and laying down the weight of it all, my Martha heart soon came to realize that at the end of the day "only one thing is necessary" (add bible reference here)

Lessons Learned from Planting a Garden

When we were kids, my dad had a huge garden, with a path going down into the middle. Once he had planted and labeled what was planted, he put up some sticks and string along the path so we would not trample down the freshly planted seeds. The garden was something that Dad so enjoyed. My dad loved green onions, and I remember rows and rows of those being planted.

The watering part was difficult because of the location of the garden. The hose could not reach the garden, so it meant filling a watering can often and walking back and forth to refresh these plants. We also realized that some plants did not do so well in the soil we had, and yet some other plants thrived in that same soil. Another thing we discovered was that something like green beans popped up and produced quickly, but something like sweet corn you needed to wait patiently for many weeks for it to produce fruit.

Gardening takes time, patience, and tons of upkeep to keep those weeds from destroying and choking out the plants; gardening is hard work! The Lord recently exposed in my heart that I'm not the patient gardener I should be. You know when you plant seeds and invest and then don't see change—don't see growth—maybe you continually try to plant seeds and water in someone life that doesn't want to grow or doesn't choose to change—maybe it's a marriage—maybe it's a prodigal child—maybe it's a love one choosing a lifestyle that is literally killing them—you plant, and you water, and nothing.

God's word reminds my gardener's heart:

> So neither the one who plants or the one who waters is anything, but
> only God who makes things grow. The one who plants and the one who

waters have one purpose and they will be rewarded according to their own labor. For we are coworkers in God's service. (1 Corinthians 3:7–9)

I'm so thankful that the Lord has been such a patient gardener with me, and in turn I need that same patience with others. I need to remember the grace, patience, and compassion He has shown me and trust him for His timing and His growing season in others. Only God can make things grow, and may I continue to water and plant and encourage as He has called me.

Comparison Is a Thief

My grandson has been in potty training mode, and the entire family is cheering him on from the sidelines—cheers, candies, phone calls, and gifts. The other day his auntie came to the house with some little cars and a squirt gun. Matthew doesn't have a squirt gun; he has never used a squirt gun. This squirt gun was a little pistol (that needed to be refilled often!). We filled the gun with water and went outside. This little pistol didn't have much pressure at all when you pulled the trigger; the water kind of trickled out.

The neighbor's little guy was outside too on this hot day, and he also had a squirt gun, but this gun was huge! This gun shot water many feet; this gun was none other than a super soaker. The boys stood within feet away from each other with just the fence separating them. Matthew was so enthralled by his gun it was like he didn't even notice the other gun … .at no time did he run over to his aunt and say, "Why didn't you get me a super soaker?"

At no time did he feel sorry for himself because he didn't have the bigger, more expensive, more powerful gun. Matthew could see how well this other boy's gun could perform, Matthew saw how far this gun shot, and yet he was so excited and thankful for this gift—this gift that was given to him and that he valued so much. He was satisfied, content and thankful for what was chosen for him. Wow, I can't tell you what that did to this grandma's heart. What an example to follow!

Immediately I thought of the many times I have compared or complained. Friends, it seems sometimes we are running this race of life, and we keep looking side to side. We are turning our heads looking at others in their race, in their lanes, and we compare, and we can feel so dissatisfied. Oh, how we can stumble when we don't fix our eyes on the lane we are in. Oh, how we can fall and feel unsatisfied when we spend so much time looking and maybe even longing to be in another lane. Oh, how important it is to fix our eyes on the finish line.

> Therefore, since we are surrounded by such a great cloud of witnesses, let us throw off everything that hinders and the sin that so easily entangles. And let us run with perseverance the race marked out for us, fixing our eyes on Jesus, the pioneer and perfecter of faith. For the joy set before him he endured the cross, scorning its shame, and sat down at the right hand of the throne of God. Consider him who endured such opposition from sinners, so that you will not grow weary and lose heart. (Hebrews 12:1–3)

What Are You Choosing to See?

I have worked in a lot of recreational activity jobs over the years. One of my favorite jobs, and most rewarding, was working in nursing homes.

The decision to send a loved one to a nursing home can come with a lot of mixed emotions and even guilt at times. The transition can be a lot more difficult when it is more of a safety issue, and the move is forced. The transition is surely a lot easier when the elderly person decides it is time to no longer live on their own.

I recalled many transitions over the years. I remember speaking to a lot of elderly gentlemen, and I think the hardest thing for them was the day they had to give up driving. I remember one man in particular who was leaving a beautiful farm and moving into a small one-bedroom place. If he wanted to go out for a drive, it meant someone else had to do it for him and with him. The days of just jumping into the car and taking off were gone.

Transitioning and giving up things you once were able to do can just be so hard. This man knew he needed to be somewhere where he needed a little more help. He chose to see now what he was missing but what was added to his life. He didn't have to make his own meals anymore, he had the company of others, and a nurse handed him his pills at the same time every day. Would he still love to be living at the farm and driving? Yes. This certainly was not what he would have chosen, but this was a great example of what he decided he would choose to see moving forward.

Who likes change? This Covid-19 pandemic has brought us is a lot of change. Some have been little changes and adjustments, and some changes have come with heartache and sacrifice—loved ones who are in nursing homes in which family cannot visit— dear ones who have passed away and no visitations and funerals—church doors and school doors are closed—new babies being born and families taking a peek through windows—weddings being postponed or altered. Who likes change, and change that seems to be forced upon us?

I was visiting with a dear friend the other day via messaging, and we were discussing how we didn't want to waste this time full of fear, anxiety, grumbling, and complaining—we wanted to see and experience what God wanted us to see and experience—and then Kath sent me this hashtag, #befruitfulinseason—wow that hit me. This is a new season, dear friends—one we certainly did not choose—but what are we choosing to see in this season? Where can we be fruitful in it?

Journeying to the Other Side

On that day, when evening had come, he said to them, "Let us go across to the other side." And leaving the crowd, they took him with them in the boat, just as he was. And other boats were with him. And a great windstorm arose, and the waves were breaking into the boat, so that the boat was already filling. But he was in the stern, asleep on the cushion. And they woke him and said to him, "Teacher, do you not care that we are perishing?" And he awoke and rebuked the wind and said to the sea, "Peace! Be still!" And the wind ceased, and there was a great calm. He said to them, "Why are you so afraid? Have you still NO faith?" And they were filled with great fear and said to one another, "Who then is this, that even the wind and the sea obey him?" (Mark 4:35–41)

When rereading this passage in God's word, I think the thing that stood out to me this time was that Jesus ushered them into this storm. The disciples were obeying what Jesus had requested of them: let's go, and they went. Did Jesus know the storm was coming? Of course he did! You can say these followers were going to be taken through a faith test.

How did they do? What do you do when the storms come crashing in?

Warren Wiersbe says:

The greatest danger was not the wind or the waves; it was the unbelief in the hearts of the disciples. Our greatest problems are within us, not around us. They had heard him teach the word and had even seen Him perform miracles, and yet they still had no faith. It was their unbelief that caused their fear, and their fear made them question whether Jesus really cared.

Reading this passage, I am reminded of a variety of storms that have come into my own life; some storms I have stayed fixed and focused on Him, and some I have floundered in such unbelief. I am also reminded how gracious, merciful, and forgiving the Lord has been to me when I have cried out in repentance and asked for forgiveness for my unbelief.

He's with you in your storm today; He will not leave you. As a follower of Christ, you are traveling with the best traveling companion ever. His name is Jesus and He is the one who has the authority to speak to your storm today: "Peace, Be Still" (Mark 4:39).

Where Are You Pitching Your Tent?

Yesterday, at church, our pastor's message was on Ephesians 2. His second point was, *But God!* Oh, don't you love those words? Doesn't your heart leap with hope reading those words? Yet my thoughts and words, many times in this journey, have been focused on *why God? When God? How God?* God's word reminds us many times, *But God!* Oh, Praise God for the *But God!* in our lives.

Three years ago this same pastor was standing by our daughter's hospital bed in the ICU as she was in critical condition and in complete organ failure. He then went down to the NICU to see our little grandson Matthew, weighing 1.7 pounds, born at twenty-seven weeks, who was also in critical condition. He prayed and wept with us that day. We cried out and called out to God. I remember looking at Pastor Kevin that day, in such a fog and struggling with such fear, and my main question was, "How, God?" I remember saying specifically to him before we prayed, "Pastor Kevin, we need so many miracles here." Both my daughter and grandson were dying. How, God, are You going to do this?

I have come to see over this circumstance and the many we have encountered and will encounter. When we camp out on the why, when, and how, it can drag us down so quickly. It isn't saying we can't be transparent when we go before the Lord and ask, "Oh, Lord, how long? Oh, Lord, why?" Look at David in the Psalms, over and over again, in his transparency, crying out to God, heart exposed. Yet David didn't camp in the why, when, and how; he camped in the *But God!*

> But I will trust you. (Psalm 55)
>
> My God in Him I will trust. (Psalm 91)
>
> But God has surely listened and has heard my prayer. (Psalm 66)

The why, when, and how, if we camp there, can take our focus off the *But God!*

Friend, I'm not sure where you are today—not aware of the burdens and troubles that are weighing you down—no idea whether you are waiting for a prodigal to return or an assessment from a doctor. But I do know, in those times, we can cry out to God like King Jehoshaphat did … when he said, "We don't know what to do *but* our eyes are fixed on *you*." (2 Chronicles 20:12, emphasis added)

The Greatest GPS

I guess you could say I'm directionally challenged at times. I can get so turned around even in a shopping mall. My husband has tried for years to teach me north, south, east, and west and not a clue on my end. On top of that, I am someone who even has questioned the GPS because it doesn't seem to be sending me in the right direction, and I go left instead of right and then within minutes place my 911 call to hubby because I'm lost. Where do you turn to for direction and guidance? Where do you go when you have hit a crossroads in your life and have no idea whether to go left or right?

The Lord has been teaching me the importance of daily laying down and handing Him my itinerary, my plans, my hopes and dreams, asking Him to guide my paths, asking Him for wisdom. God's word is packed full of guidance, scriptures that we can turn to in times of decision and our heavenly Father is so faithful to direct our steps and lead us according to His will.

> Let the morning bring me word of your unfailing love, for I have put my trust in you. Show the way I should go, for you I lift up my soul. (Psalm 143:8)

> I guide you in the way of wisdom and lead you along straight paths. (Proverbs 4:11)

> If any of you lacks wisdom, he should ask God, who gives generously to all without finding fault, and it will be given to him. (James 1:2–5)

Oh Lord, since you are my rock and my fortress for the sake of your name, lead and guide me. (Psalm 31:3)

Your word, oh Lord, is a lamp to my feet and a light for my path. (Psalm 32:8)

Trust in the Lord with all your heart and lean not on your own understanding; in all your ways submit to him, and he will make your paths straight. (Proverbs 3:5–6)

No Room

Well, the question that everyone seems to be asking these days is, "Are you ready for Christmas?"

What does the answer to that question look like for you? When do you come to the place where you can confidently say, "Yes, yes, I am ready for Christmas."

With all of the excitement and festivities of the Christmas season, it sometimes is very difficult to not get distracted, busy, and caught up with the traditions, and we can so easily lose our focus on the real reason for the season.

These things—colorful lights, cookie exchanges, office parties, Christmas parties, shopping, baking, cooking, cleaning, buying and wrapping presents, Christmas pageants at our kids'/grandkid's schools, decorating the house from top to bottom. These can all be fun and meaningful, but in our busyness, we can get very distracted and lose our focus on Christ during this season.

That little baby who came to the earth over two thousand years ago—such a humble beginning how he was literally born in a manger, in a stable because there was no room for him in the inn. We can fast-forward two thousand years later and in our hearts and busyness we can find no room for him in our jam-packed Christmas schedules … no room!

I have done it. I have gotten caught up in it and rushed through and didn't pause to remember, to recall, to reflect the difference that little baby being born that night meant. What about you? The innkeeper that evening had no room for Jesus. Is there no room in your schedule? Is there no room in your heart for Jesus? Friend, I ask you to reflect on these questions with a sense of urgency. Search your heart.

> For there is born to you this day in the city of David, a Savior who is Christ the Lord. (Luke 2:11)

Fixing Your Gaze in Battle

We will all face battles in this life; some come from out of nowhere, and some come upon us quickly. Second Chronicles 20 tells how some men came and told King Jehoshaphat: "A great multitude is coming against you (actually three armies, and they were coming quickly) Jehoshaphat was afraid and prayed and proclaimed a fast. All gathered to seek help from the Lord (although he was shaken and afraid, Jehoshaphat didn't focus on the enemy, He focused on God. When shaken and afraid, where do you focus?" (2 Chronicles 20:3)

He prayed, "O Lord, God of our fathers, are you not God in heaven? You rule over all the kingdoms of the nations. In your hand are power and might, so that none is able to withstand you. Did you not, our God, drive out the inhabitants of this land … we cry out to you in our affliction, knowing you will hear and save."

Jehoshaphat reminds himself of who God is and what God has done, which is such a great reminder and example when we are walking through a battle. Jehoshaphat continues "For we are powerless against this great multitude that is coming against us. We do not know what to do, but our eyes are on you." Jehoshaphat realized he could do nothing without God. He was seeking the only one who could do something and was showing his people where his true strength came from. His worried heart totally surrendered to God and the Lord said "Do not be afraid and do not be dismayed at this great multitude for the battle is not yours but God's. You will not need to fight in this battle. Do not be afraid and do not be dismayed. Tomorrow go out against them, and the Lord will be with you" (2 Chronicles 20:16) Then Jehoshaphat and His people stood up to praise the Lord with a very loud voice.

Jehoshaphat and all the people had turned their fear into loud worship to their God ... they were fully surrendered and worshiping the *one* who was going to take on this battle, and they rose early in the morning and went into battle singing and giving thanks to the Lord. "And when they began to sing and praise, the Lord set an ambush against the enemies" (2 Chronicles 20:22).

When we seek God, He will speak into our circumstance/our trial; He directs, He guides, He gives wisdom, and He delivers.

Thankful Thinking Is Key

The other day I found myself in a situation that I knew was starting to spiral quickly in my mind. The anxiety, fear, and worry started to creep in, and the more I dwelled on the circumstance, the more the anxiety grew. I knew immediately that I needed to stop, drop, and pray! I recalled God's word, remembering what the apostle Paul had written about the importance of thanksgiving in Philippians 4:6–7:

> Do not be anxious about anything, but in every situation, by prayer and petition with thanksgiving, present your requests to God, and the peace of God, which transcends all understanding, will guard your hearts and your minds in Christ Jesus.

I dwelled on God's promises; I redirected my gaze and my thoughts to thanksgiving, and as God's word promised, a peace came. I was reminded of past storms in my life where God ushered us onto dry land, and I recalled hopeless situations where God miraculously turned it all around. I was reminded of the character of my heavenly Father.

Thanksgiving is certainly a choice you make. Thanksgiving is so key because it pauses the anxious mind and takes the thoughts to one of thanksgiving. You can't be thinking two thoughts at once. The choice of thanksgiving has your mind recall and remember. The choice of thanksgiving redirects my heart and eyes to Christ and not my circumstances.

When anxious thoughts or difficult circumstances present themselves, does thanksgiving enter your mind?

Looking in the Rearview Mirror

There can be some mixed messages out there about looking back. When is it good to look back, and when is it not?

I recently did an in-depth study on forgiveness. What I learned is that there are a lot of bitter roots growing deeper and deeper, causing our hearts to harden, as we keep looking back to the past. During this study, I read many verses regarding leaving the past in the past and pressing onward. We are not to call to mind the former things of the past, instead forgetting what lies behind and reaching forward (Philippians 3:13–14; Isaiah 43:18–19, 25).

One early morning, on my way to worship practice, I was captivated by what was going on behind me. Darkness was in front of me, but when I looked in my rearview mirror the most glorious sun was rising. The darkness was fleeing, and the most beautiful shades of yellow and orange were emerging. I couldn't stop looking back. The sun was rising, and it was so beautiful. In front of me was darkness, but looking in the rearview mirror, hope was emerging.

I believe that in those times when we are in a storm, when it seems the darkest, we need to look back and recall the Lord. We need to remind ourselves how He has been faithful and has carried us in the past, and He will continue to carry us. We need to look back at His faithfulness to us in the past and remind ourselves that that same faithful Father has not and will not leave us. I believe that in these times, it does the heart good to recall, bring to memory, and dwell on the goodness of a faithful, loving, dependable, and sovereign God who is holding us in the palm of His hand.

> Ah Sovereign Lord, you have made the heavens and the earth by your great power and outstretched arm. Nothing is too hard for you. (Jeremiah 32:17)

Are You Hearing or Listening?

In Charles Stanley's book *Prayer: The Ultimate Conservation,* he tells this story.

> On a trip I once took to Israel, I witnessed one of the most powerful illustrations of listening to our Good Shepherd that I have ever seen. I will never forget it. The evening sun was setting, and two shepherds approached a nearby well with their flocks. For approximately 20 minutes the two men chatted while their sheep mingled and roamed about. The animals wandered everywhere. Soon you could not tell one group from the other because they were so interspersed and scattered throughout the countryside. Then something extraordinary happened. One of the shepherds turned around, quietly called out a command, and started walking away. Instantly, those two flocks separated. The sheep recognized their master's voice and as he made his way up the hill side, they streamed in from every direction to follow him. They knew exactly what to do and were motivated to obey.

If you are a parent of a teen or a toddler, you discover very quickly there can be a huge difference between hearing and listening, and then going from listening to obeying is a whole other story. That listening and obeying combo is when we parents do high fives, dance around the kitchen, and begin thanking God because they are finally getting it!

What about you? Who are you listening to? Who or what have you been following? Child of God, how are you doing with the listening, obeying, and following? This world has every distraction imaginable—lots of voices giving input and direction, lots of noise and multiple paths to choose from. Here is some encouragement from God's word for you today:

> The gatekeeper opens the gate for him, and the sheep listen to his voice. He calls his own sheep by name and leads them out. When he has brought out all his own, he goes on ahead of them, and his sheep follow him because they know his voice. But they will never follow a stranger; in fact, they will run away from him because they do not recognize a stranger's voice. (John 10:3–5 NIV)

> I am the good shepherd; I know my sheep and my sheep know me—just as the Father knows me and I know the Father—and I lay down my life for the sheep. (John 10:15 NIV)

Waiting to Hear from You

My husband, Dan, is an avid outdoorsman, and fall is certainly his favorite time of the year. This fall, Danny had the opportunity to go moose hunting with a few friends up north (approximately twenty-four hours from home, because that is where the big moose are, I'm told!). When the men arrived at their main destination, they would unload trucks and then canoe into the prime hunting ground.

Danny warned me that he was most certain there would be *no* cell reception where they were going. It has been twelve days since I have spoken to Danny, and, oh, how I miss hearing his voice. I have things written down to tell him when he calls. I can't wait to hear his stories and hear whether they were successful in the hunt. I have been carrying my phone with me everywhere (yes, even to the bathroom) just in case he would call. Longing and waiting to hear his voice.

This got me thinking about our heavenly Father—how often is He waiting for us to call? How often is He waiting for us to come and talk through or invite Him into our decision-making? How often does He see us spinning in confusion and waiting for us to call and ask for wisdom in the day to day? How often does He just want to hear, "Thank you, Lord," for the everyday blessings or just hearing us calling on His name in our praise—worshipping and bringing glory and honor to Him? There was a time in my life that my calls to Him were either when there was an emergency, or I needed something. And once the crisis had passed or the blessing was given—silence—I didn't call!

Oh friends, I am learning to take full advantage of the ability to be able to call on Him—I can call on Him whenever and for whatever. The reception is always clear, full bars, and He always answers. If you haven't called Him—will you?

He is longing to hear from you!

What to Wear?

If you are like me, you have entertained yourself with makeover shows, specifically, what you should or shouldn't be wearing. I find they can be educational and also very amusing at times. The premise of the show is that a loved one nominates someone they believe needs a makeover. If chosen, that person's closet doors are flung wide open and critiqued, which often results in many items being pitched in the garbage.

I realized today, when studying Colossians 3, that Paul is kind of doing the same thing here to a degree. I realize some of you theologians may question my research in finding Paul to be the inventor of makeover shows, but hear me out. Paul is confronting believers and challenging them with what they should not be wearing and reminding them of what they should be wearing.

Let's read Colossians 3:7–15 together:

> You used to walk in these ways, in the life you once lived. But now you must also rid yourselves of all such things as these: anger, rage, malice, slander, and filthy language from your lips. Do not lie to each other, since you have taken off your old self with its practices and have put on the new self, which is being renewed in knowledge in the image of its Creator. Here there is no Gentile or Jew, circumcised or uncircumcised, barbarian, Scythian, slave or free, but Christ is all, and is in all. Therefore, as God's chosen people, holy and dearly loved, clothe yourselves with compassion, kindness, humility, gentleness and patience. Bear with each other and forgive one another if any of you has a grievance against someone. Forgive as the Lord forgave you. And over all these virtues put

on love, which binds them all together in perfect unity. Let the peace of Christ rule in your hearts, since as members of one body you were called to peace. And be thankful.

Oh friends, how we need the Lord's help to put on compassion, gentleness, love, and patience. It seems that sometimes the comfy clothes in our closets are the anger, slander, bitterness, and the pointing fingers. May you be challenged, as I have been reading this scripture, of what *not* to wear!

Printed in the United States
by Baker & Taylor Publisher Services